In t

MW01121958

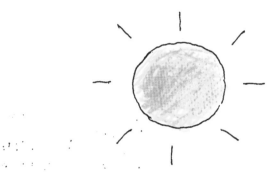

Written by Jenny Feely
Illustrations by Alex Stitt

sundance

Contents

A picture of stars circling
in the sky, taken by time
exposure.

4

Introduction

We live on the **planet** Earth.
Earth is in space. Space looks empty,
but it is not.

When you look up at the sky,
you are looking into space.

This photograph of planet Earth
was taken from a satellite in space.

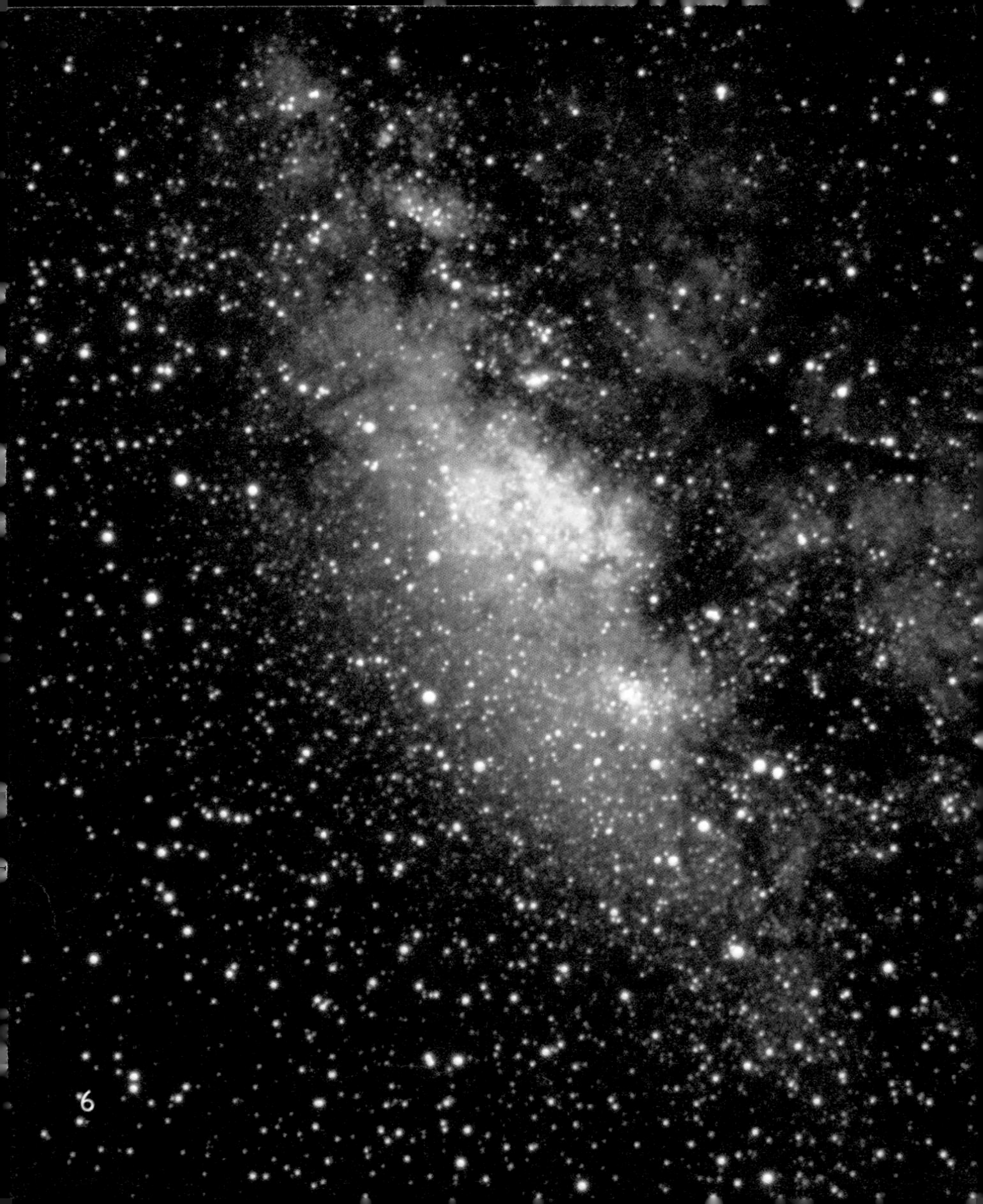
6

The Milky Way

Earth is in a part of space called the Milky Way. The Milky Way is a galaxy. Galaxies are made up of millions and millions of stars. No one knows how many galaxies there are.

Our sun, the moon, and all of the stars that we can see in the sky are part of the Milky Way.

This picture of the Milky Way was taken using a telescope. From Earth, the Milky Way looks like a misty patch of light in the sky.

The Sun

The sun is a very large ball of burning **gas**, and it creates huge amounts of heat and light. The sun is so hot that its heat reaches Earth, even though it is 93 million miles away. The sun's light is so bright, it lights up Earth.

The sun is always in the sky. You cannot always see it, but it is always there.

The sun's light is so bright that it can hurt your eyes. You should never look directly at the sun through sunglasses, binoculars, or a telescope.

Day and Night

Each day the sun seems to be moving across the sky. But it's not. Earth is moving. Every 24 hours, Earth makes one complete turn, or spin. This causes night and day.

Dawn
for the duck

Noon

Dusk

Night

The Moon

The moon is a large rock that moves around Earth. The moon does not make its own light. The sun lights up part of the moon, and we can see the moon in the night sky.

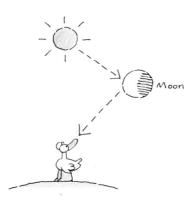

As the moon moves around Earth each month, it seems to change shape.

The moon reflects light from the sun. It is this light we can see in the night sky.

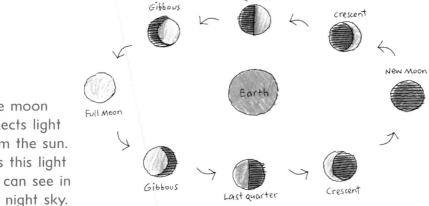

13

corona

14

Solar Eclipse

Sometimes the moon
is between the sun
and Earth, and it blocks
the sunlight.

When this happens,
it is called a solar
eclipse. Suddenly it
becomes dark for a short
while during the day.

All that can be seen
of the sun is a bright
circle of light called
a corona.

A solar eclipse.

16

Stars

There are many stars in space. Stars are balls of burning gas, like the sun.

Most stars seem small because they are far away from Earth. But they are really very big.

The biggest stars are called super giants. Super giants can be 100 times bigger than the sun, and the sun is 100 times bigger than Earth.

The smallest stars are called white dwarfs. Even the smallest white dwarf is bigger than Earth.

Stars are not all the same color.
Red stars are the coolest stars.
Bluish stars are the hottest.

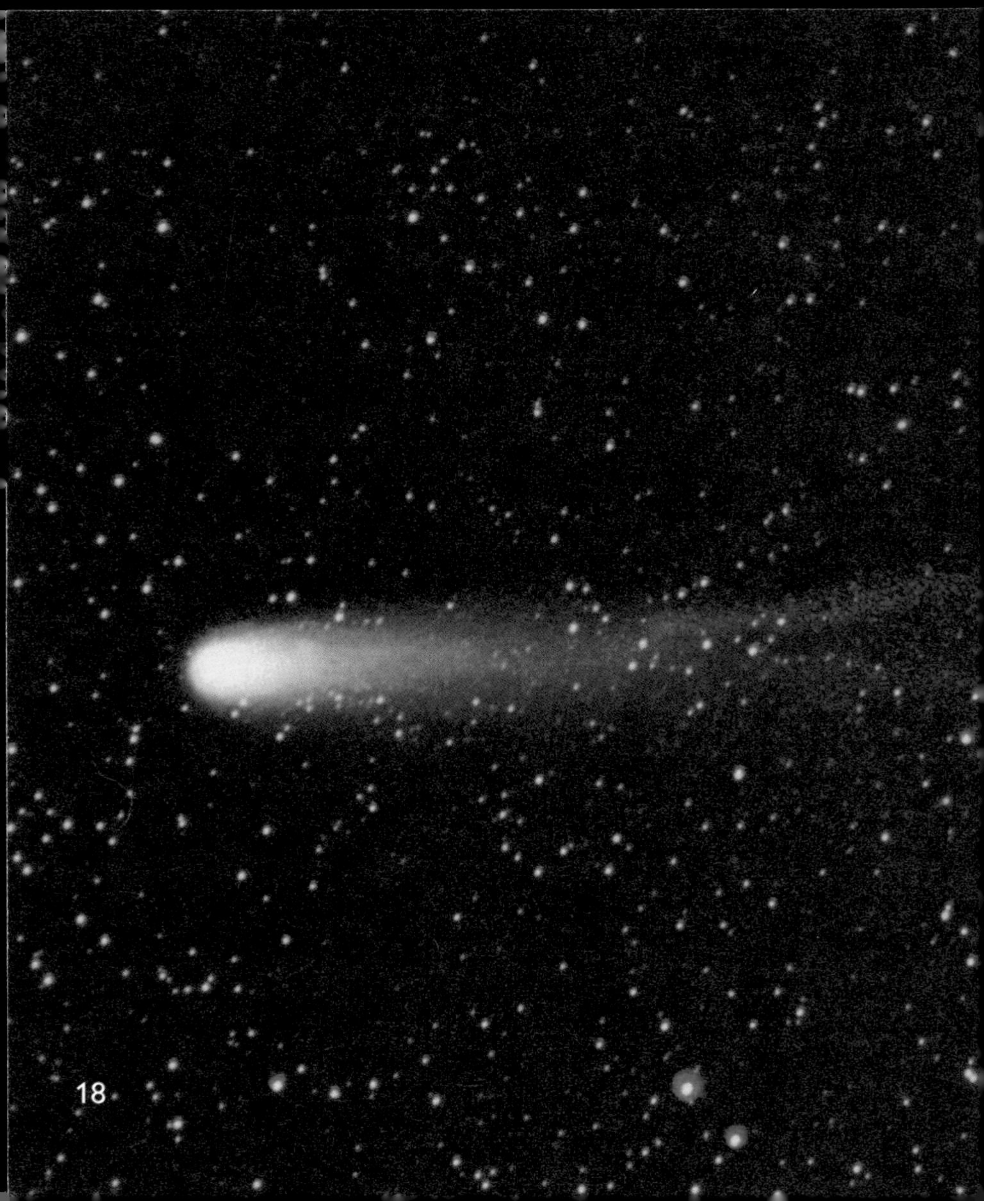

Comets

Comets are balls of ice and rock that travel around the sun.

The sun heats the comet. A cloud of gas and dust forms.

Strong winds from the sun blow the gas and dust away from the comet. The gas and dust form the comet's tail.

Halley's Comet can be seen from Earth once every 76 years. It was last seen in 1986.

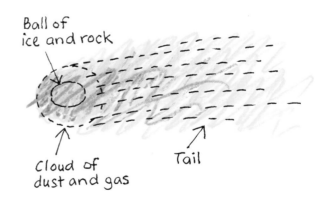

Ball of ice and rock

Cloud of dust and gas

Tail

Planets

Earth is one of nine planets that move around the sun.

Mercury, Venus, Earth, and Mars are made of rock. They are called the rocky planets.

Jupiter, Saturn, Uranus, and Neptune are made of gas. These planets are huge. They are called the gas giants.

Pluto is small. It is made of rock and ice. Pluto is called an ice dwarf.

Jupiter is one of the 9 planets that move around the sun. It is about 11 times bigger than Earth.

Finding Out About Space

There are many things in space we cannot see with our eyes.

Scientists who study space are called astronomers. They use **telescopes** and **space probes** to collect information about space.

Some telescopes are on Earth. Other telescopes are sent into space. These telescopes send information back to Earth. Sometimes robots are sent into space to collect information as well.

The Hubble telescope is in space.
This telescope can be used
to observe stars more closely.

Glossary

gas	a substance that is not a solid or a liquid
planet	a large object that moves around a star or a sun
space probes	machines that travel through space to collect information about space
telescopes	tools that help people to see things that are very far away